BRED
FROM THE
EYES OF A
WOLF

D1558164

Bred from the Eyes of a Wolf © 2018 Kim Kyung Ju
English translation © 2018 Jake Levine

This book is published with the support of the Literature
Translation Institute of Korea (LTI Korea)

Published by Plays Inverse Press
Pittsburgh, PA
www.playsinverse.com

ISBN-13: 978-0-9997247-4-3

First Printing: September 2018
Cover design by Andrew Shuta
Page design by Tyler Crumrine
Printed in the U.S.A.

**PLAYS
INVERSE**

BRED
FROM THE
EYES OF A
WOLF

KIM KYUNG JU

TRANSLATED BY JAKE LEVINE

PLAYS INVERSE PRESS
PITTSBURGH, PA
2018

NOTES ON TRANSLATION

There has been a lot of fuss about the difficulty of translating Korean to English and English to Korean. In that conversation, the Korean language has been called things like "repetitive" and English very "precise." I find this kind of boiled-down generalization both reductive and orientalist. Like literatures of all languages, there are many different styles of writing in Korean. In translating Kim Kyung Ju, one of the most linguistically imaginative and difficult writers in Korea, it is often impossible to find an English equivalent or substitute to match the precision of his language. He often mixes and experiments with combinations of hanja (Chinese characters) in order to create words which don't exist. Additionally, the richness of punning and onomatopoeia in the Korean language is something that is either lost or maimed in English. Because of this loss, I have often tried to substitute or create maximalist interpretations to offer the reader some semblance of the magic of the original. However, this method is not without its faults. If the playfulness of poetic speech performs the magic of creating a multiplicity of readings, then the translator has the awkward task of picking up all the multiple-readings and awkwardly forcing them into some mangled, second-rate object. And I guess this is the heart of the problem. If the poet is like a magician, the translator is more like the ventriloquist's dummy. Even though the words appear to be falling out of my mouth, we all know it is not me who is really doing the talking.

Bred from the Eyes of a Wolf originally comes from a poem found in the English translation of Kim's first book of poetry, *I Am a Season That Does Not Exist in the World* (Black Ocean, 2016). Many sequences in all of Kim's plays borrow lines and scenes that appear in his poetry. This creates a labyrinthine experience for both reader and translator, one that becomes all the more rich and layered the more familiar one is with Kim's body of work. This also is why Kim does not distinguish between genres. Poets build their own universe of meaning with a unique language, a universe that is expansive and dynamic enough for multiple bodies of work to populate and grow in. This is also why it is not the stories or speech of his characters, but the organic environment that continues to grow and haunt after the last page has been finished.

As is customary at the end of a translator's note, I wanted to give thanks to some people without whom this book could not have been completed. First, thank you to Hedgie Choi who helped translate the original manuscript. Thanks to the people at the Literature Translation Institute of Korea for their support, and especially to Claire Kyung Jin who has tirelessly promoted my translation work. Thanks to Tyler Crumrine for his editorial vision and thanks to one of my oldest partners in crime, Andrew Shuta, for making the cover design. And lastly, I want to thank my wolf-brother Kim Kyung Ju. Like the howl of a pack of wolves after the kill, I hear your echo inside my speech.

— Jake Levine, 2017

PREFACE

It is possible that humans on stage appear as wolves.

And it is possible that wolves on stage appear as humans.

TIME

In an age of collision and blended time,
after the atomic war,
species intermingle
and resemble other species.

CAST

Mom

Son

Woman

Policeman 1

Policeman 2

Wolf Cub 1*

Wolf Cub 2*

---

*Dolls

SETTING

In a dark forest,
inside the hulk of a dead tree,
pitch black, gloomy,

here and there roots dangle.

Drip, drop.

Tears of water
splash down.

Spit dribbles down
from the open mouths of bats
hanging from the ceiling.

Drop, drip.

Outside the window,
livers clustered together
are dangling
in the dark
from a red tree.

Taxidermied animals
on the wall
hang off hooks.

Devices for experiments.
Glass bottles filled with internal organs
inside a cabinet smeared with blood.

Like a butcher in a butcher's shop,
like a scientist in a lab,

drip, drip, drop.

Pacing back and forth,
someone outside
grabs the handle to the door
and turns the knob.

Drip, water drops.

Drip, drop.

ACT ONE

Mom wears leather gloves and a butcher's apron. Sitting down, she is stuffing dead animals.

Wads of cotton and iron spikes are piled next to the refrigerator and TV.

Son wears a shirt with stretched out baggy sleeves (the bigger the better, to emphasize he has no arms). He feebly enters the scene.

Son puts his face up to Mom's anus. His nostrils flare out.

Mom:
Son,
what are you doing home?

Son:
Shit,
somehow I ended up here again.

Mom:
You shouldn't just show up
without calling.
What if my boyfriend was here?
That would've been a big deal, no?

Son:
I didn't have the money to call.

Mom:
If you're here to strangle me
and steal my money again,
it'd be better to give up right now.
I'm broke.

Silence.

Mom:
By the way, how did you find your way here?

Son:
I caught a whiff of your excrement.
So I followed it, you know, just in case.

I'm good at smelling
the smells
you leave behind.

   Silence.

Mom:
What did you think you'd find?
My corpse, wasted away, lying here
with its mouth open?

That expression you're making,
is that really what you expected to see?

Are you surprised I'm not dead?

Don't you think you've gone too far this time?
Actually looking for me?

   Silence.

Mom: *(Surveying Son's body:)*
And what happened to your arm? Your one good arm?
It's gone.

   Son rocks the rocking chair.

Son:
Y'know, I had an accident.

Mom:
Accident? What accident?

Tell me! Did you step in a trap?

Son:
Mom, you know how life is.

Son rocks the rocking chair.

Mom:
Right! Just an accident.
If only I hadn't eaten those things
when I was carrying you…

Son:
God… not that story again.
Mom,
can't you stop with that story?

Mom:
Son,
it's the first time in two years that we meet…

Son:
Okay, go ahead,
you want to tell me about the time,
the time you had morning sickness…

Mom:
Morning sickness, right!
Those mamushi snakes
your father brought me,
I knew I shouldn't have eaten them.

Son:
Dad wanted to feed you
sprightly birds, but no…
You're probably
the only person in the world
who ever craved live vipers
because you got pregnant.

Mom:
If only I had known
that the baby mamushi
inside that mother mamushi
would tear out of its mother's body
and eat your arm…

Son:
Mom, how many times have I told you?
That's just what you *assumed* happened.

Mom:
It must have been scary…
Every night I could feel that snake
sleeping, grinding
its teeth inside my gut.

Son:
That was just a nightmare.
I dreamed the same thing
when I was inside you.

Mom:
Son, that day
I heard your screams crystal clear.
They came from the inside of my body.

Son:
I remember.
I couldn't even speak
near the mamushi.
I was too afraid.

Mom:
I remember
you inside me.
Yawning twice a day,
peeing three times,
and at night

you practiced crying
until daybreak. Yes.
Every ten seconds you cried.

Son:
Actually, funny,
it's been so long since then...
I really can't remember now.

Mom:
That's right.
It must have been dark inside there. Gloomy even.
And I don't remember it that well either.
The outside world sure is better, isn't it?
Better than inside that dark belly.

While you were in my stomach
you would knock on the walls
with your small fists.

The noise was so loud that
I was too embarrassed
to walk around the forest.

 Silence.

But your father, he said,

Do you hear that?
A bird is flying around
in your stomach.

It made him so happy.

 Son suddenly looks forlorn,
 looking around at all the stuffed animals in the house.

Son:
Mom, do you still

take dead animals and bring them here?

Mom:
I wish.
I don't know if they all have gone extinct or not but
lately I haven't even seen any of them. Not even a trace.

It's even hard to find
roadkill or
animals killed in traps.

I swear, it won't be long and
my anus is going to shrivel up
and I'm going to die just like that.
Death by shrivelled anus.

You know, sometimes I think it would be better
to get stuffed and taxidermied
rather than go on
living with this hunger.

Son:
You're right.
I know life sure would be better
if I'd already been stuffed.

Mom: *(Looking at him like he's pathetic:)*
At least animals that have been taxidermied
can be sold outside.

   Mom looks concerned.

Are you not eating these days?

   Son shakes his head from side to side.

Son: *(Looking at the stuffed animals:)*
Mom,
I feel like their eyeballs

are pointed at us.

Mom:
When I stuff an animal
the first thing I do is carve out the eyes.
Eyes are so unpleasant.

You know something funny,
that's the same thought I think
when I look
at your eyes too.

Son:
Don't they rot?

Mom:
I'm very thorough about the preservation process.

Son:
You dig out
every last inch of
intestine
before stuffing the body with cotton.

Mom: *(Laughing:)*
I bet all these lovely creatures are warmer now
and softer inside
than they ever were when they were alive.

> *Mom gets up and puts the taxidermied animal in the refrigerator.*
> *She returns with a cup of tap water.*

Son:
They're rotting.

Mom:
Taxidermied animals don't rot.
Never.

Son:
They don't cry?

Mom:
How awful
would it be
if a taxidermied animal cried?

Son:
Yeah.
No animal can escape its fate.
If it is going to be stuffed, it gets stuffed.
My arm
hasn't been stuffed yet, has it?
Where did it go?

Mom:
Again,
bringing up this business with your arm.
Like I told you before, your arm isn't here.

Son:
My arm is here.

Mom:
You dumb shit.
You come back after two years
and that's all
you can say to me?

You know that woman who looks
nothing like you
that lives inside me? Who knows
what she might do? Anytime. Anytime.
She might come out
and report you.

Son:
I only came here because I want to find my arms.

Mom:
Stop talking
about your damn arms.
We don't have that kind of thing
here.

Son:
One arm is here. I know it is.
Here!

Mom throws the cup of water in Son's face.

Mom:
I said stop!

Son:
Listen carefully.
Do you hear something?
Do you hear it?

Mom:
I'm begging you.
Stop it!

"Squeak squeak, squeak squeak."

Mom:
Ugh! Rats!
Rats! Swarming.
Everywhere!
Fucking. Multiplying.
Traps. Set traps.
I hate rats. Hate rats.

Mom lays rat traps here and there.
Son paces nervously.

Silence.

Mom:
Your hair has grown so long.
Since you've been away, really
you've become quite a beast.

Come here.

Take a seat.

Son:
Mom... I don't want to.
I need my natural camouflage
to adapt to the wild.

Mom:
Come on. Come here and sit.

Now!

> *Son sinks into the rocking chair.*

> *Mom, cutting Son's hair with shears,
> accidentally cuts Son's ear.*

Son: *(Baring his teeth:)*

> ::Wolf howl!::

Mom:
Go ahead,
howl while you're still young
and there is still some wildness left in you.
Whatever emotions you're feeling, go on,
express yourself.
Flash those sharp canines.
Yes, as much as you want, as long as you never,
never suggest,
that you'll bite your owner.

Remember, to be obedient is best.

Nobody
is quick to forgive
betrayal.

Because anyone that is
accepting of you
has got to be,
well, well, let's just say
they've got to be
quite
e.x.p.e.r.i.m.e.n.t.a.l.

Son:
No! I would never!

Mom:
Oh?

Mom makes a cut on the other ear.

Son:
::Wolf howl!::

Mom:
I'm sorry.
It's just your ears are always in the way.
If only they weren't there,
cutting your hair would be so easy.

Son:
Mom!

Mom:
Okay okay.
I'll be careful.

Mom scissors carefully.

What kind of woman did you meet
this time around
that it took you so long to come back?

Son:
A woman that couldn't see things
in front of her face.

Mom:
You mean she was blind?

Son:
Yes.
In front of that woman
I pulled down my pants
and said,
Go on, touch it.

> *Mom smiles, imitating snipping something in the air with her scissors.*

Mom:
Oh be quiet!
You didn't give it
to that woman, did you?

Son:
No.
I didn't give it.
Not to her.

Mom:
That's good.
It's been so hard to keep *it* around.
If you're just going to give *it* to some woman you met on the street
you should give *it* to me instead.

> *Pause.*

So...
What kind of girl is she?
I mean, being blind
is not really that big of a problem, is it?

Did you, you know,
kiss?

Son:
It was the first time
I put my tongue into
the mouth of another.

Mom: *(Laughing:)*
Not me.

Son:
I went to her hometown
to meet her family
and it turned out
she was not the only one.
The whole family couldn't see in front of their faces.

Mom:
Shame!
It's depressing that they weren't able to take a peek
at your handsome face.
Of course if they did see
they might have become overwhelmed
at the sight
and fainted on the spot.

Son:
Their faces were pointed in the direction of the TV,
and when I entered
they came
toward me,
guiding themselves by
pawing the wall.

Mom:
Really?

Son:
They all took turns
feeling my face. They did this for a long time.
Then they gave me a place near the heat
and told me
Sit and make yourself comfortable.
Then
they reached forward with their two paws
and requested I shake.

Mom:
How kind of them.

They must have
warmly grabbed your paw
and explained to you the various ways in which
one carries oneself through this difficult life.

Son:
Mom! It was terrible!

I've never shaken a paw in my life!

Mom:
That's right!

You've never had a shake.

But that's no reason
for poor manners.

So what did you do?

Son: *(Lifting his two legs while sitting in the chair:)*
I lifted my rears
and politely placed them

on top of their front paws.

Mom: *(Taking his two rears in her front paws:)*
You did well.
Rear paws, front paws,
it's all the same.

Son:
They gently took my rears
and put them on the floor
and said
they'd like to squeeze
one of my front paws.

Mom:
Yes.
I've heard families that live happily together
often hold
each other's paws.

Son: *(Lifting a foot:)*
Yes. I heard that too.
So
I lifted my foot many times
and put it politely
in their paws.

Mom: *(Taking the foot in her paws:)*
Politely?

Son:
Yes. Politely.

But they told me to break up with their daughter.

They said I should leave
their house
immediately.

Mom:
Leave?
What do you mean?

They treated you, a boy they've never met,
in this way?

Son:
They said
their daughter
needed a man
who could wipe away
their daughter's tears.

Mom:
Fucking savages!

What did you say?

Son:
Of course I said that I've been
wiping her tears with these two feet
all this time.

Mom:
Don't just say you've been doing it!

You have to say that
you can demonstrate
in front of them.
On the spot if necessary.

Son:
Ah!
I didn't think of that.
I've still got
a long way to go
until I am as smart as you.

Mom:
God, idiot.
So you got rejected
this time around too?

Son:
They asked
when the world becomes difficult
how would we survive
after we start living together.

Mom:
You should've said
you'd think it over slowly
and reply to them
by letter or by email.

Son:
They told me to answer
immediately.

Mom:
You should've answered
like a warrior.

Son:
I told them that
I say to her
that I am not
crying
when I am crying
and
when she
is crying
I tell her
that I don't see
her tears.

That's how I responded.

Mom:
Excellent answer, but
if they had decided to take you in as their son-in-law
they'd most likely die
with their eyes wide open, right?

Pause.

Mom:
So, did you have to break up with her?

Was it because you have no arms?

Son:
You could put it that way.

Mom:
God, how could you give up so easy?

You've got to get on your hands and feet and beg.

Grab and squeeze their legs until they give in.

Son:
Mom,
why did you never teach me how to do that?

Mom:
Son, you've got to adapt to the situation!

Next time, if need be,
beg until your feet become your hands.

You are so weak,
you wouldn't even be able to convince a stew
to let you have a sip of its soup.

Son:
Even if I don't get

a dribble of soup,
I think from now on
it would be wise if I try to meet
a woman who doesn't cry.

Mom:
There is no such thing as that kind of woman.

Son:
Then I must meet a woman
who can wipe
away her tears independently,
without the aid of a man.

Mom:
A woman like that
would never be with a cripple
like you.

Son:
Cripple? Fine, whatever mother.

But tell me, why did her family
begin to cry when they heard
the tap of my claws on the ground
as I left their house?

Mom gets another cup of tap water, searches around for the remote, and turns on the TV.

Mom:
It's not you.

It's because they were watching a TV show.

Watching TV is the only time a family sits around
and cries together.

Son:
They were scared so they
crammed themselves into a corner.

They huddled
like maggots.

Mom:
What kind of voice did you make?

Son:
Me? I roared. I roared loud.

Mom: *(Throwing the remote aside:)*
Son! Come and give your mom a hug!

Mom embraces Son.

Mom:
Squeeze!

Son:
Mom, why're you acting like this? Mom!

Mom: *(Smiling:)*
So you went up to them
and wiped their tears for them.
Didn't you?

Son:
Damn right.
I told them all to lay down on their sides
and I wiped their tears with my two feet.

Mom:
I'm so proud of you.

My son! My son!

Even if they didn't see it coming,
you have to make sure they are completely dead.

You took care of it, right?

Son:
Is there still blood on my teeth?

Mom:
Say "ah".......

    Son opens his mouth.

Son:
Ah.......

Mom:
A little bit of flesh is stuck
on your third canine.

So what did you do with their leftovers?

Son:
I threw them to the
neighborhood dogs.

Mom:
I'm so proud of you.

My son! My son!

    Mom pulls Son in for an embrace.
    Son suddenly looks forlorn.

Mom:
What's the matter child?

Son:
It's nothing.

While I was away
I only ate uncooked things.

So my head hurts.

That's all.

Mom: *(Giving him water to drink:)*
Rinse out your mouth.

> *Son rinses out his mouth.*
> *Son flops onto the floor.*
>
> *Mom takes a wad of money out of the refrigerator and hides it in*
> *the floor and gives Son another glass of water.*
>
> *After a moment Mom glances at Son.*

Mom:
Son, isn't it time
you stopped wandering around?

You know,
got a job, started a family?

Son:
Look at me mother!

What kind of work can someone like me do?

Mom:
What's wrong with you, huh?
You're just missing two arms. That's all.
Aside from that
you're a vision of normalcy.

Don't get discouraged.
There's plenty of jobs
that can be done

with nothing but a mouth.

Son:
I can't con people again.
I'll get found out like the last time.

Mom takes a hammer from out of the toolbox.

Mom:
You're just out of practice.
If you just practice
and don't run away like the last time,
you'll be fine.

If you don't have arms,
you've got to live by the strength of your tongue.

Son:
Mom…

Mom:
Yes?

Son:
I can't do any work anymore. I just can't…

Mom:
How do you mean?

This is fucking shocking! How shocking!

Do you plan for your mother to starve?!

Perhaps you should intentionally get into an accident.

You know, injury fraud isn't such a bad idea.

If a cripple like you gets hit by a car
people are likely to have sympathy.

After you get hit
you must scream in pain
and then negotiate a settlement.

When you are laid up in the hospital
you can count the money
with your leftover toes.

> *Son puts his foot down on a rock.*
> *As Mom brings the hammer down toward his foot,*
> *Son pulls his foot out of the way at the last second.*

Son:
Wait!

Mom:
What?

Son:
Do you really think I'll be able to count money with my toes?

Mom:
If you lick the money and get it nice and spitty,
it'll be easy.

> *Son puts his foot down on a rock.*
> *The hammer comes down, but he pulls his foot out of the way at*
> *the very last second.*
> *Mom chucks the hammer.*

Son:
You know all that money we got last time?

Mom:
It got used up two years ago.

Son:
What about the money
I earned by rolling balls around

with my tongue
at the circus?

Mom:
I used it up
on admission tickets
to watch you roll balls around
with your tongue
at the circus.

Son:
What about the money
I earned carrying small light bulbs
in my mouth
at the factory?

Mom:
I used it
to get new light bulbs
for the house.

Son:
Mom,
there aren't many jobs
you can do without two arms.

Mom:
You talk
just like
your father when he was young.

Just like,
just like him.

Always running around behind some woman's asshole.

Destined to be poor.

Son:
I have a father?

Mom:
There is no such thing
as a fatherless person.

The one that wanders
in the mountains out there,
whoever that man is, he
is your father.

Son: *(Looking out the window:)*
Father, are you out there?

Mom:
Your father lives a life of forest wandering.

Son:
Because he is a dreamer?

Mom:
Your father is a poet. Didn't you know?

Son:
Mom, you know
I've never seen
my dad.

Mom:
At night, at the top of the hill
he sticks his asshole in the air
and with his neck stretched way out,
he wails.

Son:
Like a ghost?

Mom:
If ghosts cry
because they long for things
they miss in this world,
then I guess you could say he is like a ghost.

Son looks out the window and stretches out a long wail.

Mom:
What the hell?

Quit it right now!

A beast that wails inside the house?

Are you a savage?! How embarrassing!

Son: *(Giggling:)*
I bet dad also
sniffed around your asshole.

Mom: *(Smiling:)*
Of course your dad
sniffed around my asshole.

Son:
Mom!!! I can't believe dad did that, no!

Mom:
As a sign of our loneliness
we spread our assholes out
and showed them to each other.

Son: *(Laughing hysterically:)*
Mom! Stop it. Stop it.

I can't take it.

I can't

stop
laughing.

Mom:
I left home at nineteen
and didn't have anywhere to go.

I used to sleep outside, in the forest.

One night your father came over to me
and rubbed his nose
around my anus.

Then
he whispered
into my ear.

Son:
Heehee, what did he say?

Mom:
You, me…. Together…. Let's live .. . .

Son:
You totally fell for it.

Mom:
He looked so lonely.

Every night he searched me out
and licked
my asshole.

Son:
What a beast!

Mom:
Beasts, that's how they are.

When they are lonely
they display
their assholes
to each other.

Son:
You know, this is a principle
I too have come to understand
through shitting.

Mom:
I see. Now that you've been out there in the world,
you've learned how to breathe
through your asshole.

Son:
And then what happened between you two?

Mom:
Eventually we
ended up shitting in the same place.

Because
living together means
to shit
in the same place.

Then, we spent thirty years
drooling diligently, moving you and your sisters
around with our mouths, eventually
ending up here.

    Pause.

Mom:
Your dad
lost nine of his toes
in the jerky factory
trying to keep us fed.

Son:
One a year!

Mom:
Yes, and sometimes one every six months.

Son:
That was your idea, wasn't it!

To have dad put his foot
into the machines.

Claim injury compensation.

You know, even now it seems
like such an excellent plan.

   Mom is pleased, shakes her ass.

Mom:
Yes.

If it wasn't for that plan
we would have all
starved to death.

Son:
Mom,
but what about me?

Born without an arm, losing another,
how will I ever be able
to contribute to this family?

Mom:
Think very hard.
I bet there is
something you can do.

Son:
Think, think, I must think
of a good scheme.

Mom:
That's right, a good scheme!

But son,
you know you could die
scheming your own schemes.

Because that's life.

Son:
What do you mean? I don't understand.

Mom:
Before he left
your father
wrote that down on a piece of paper.

You could die scheming your own schemes.

He wrote it down on a piece
of paper and left it on the table
along with one of his molars.

Son:
Dad said that and left?

Mom:
Yes.

Your father
left behind those words.

Those words.

Who knows what the hell they mean.

And then he left this house.

Son:
Why?

Mom:
It's hard enough to make ends meet
with just one cripple
in a house. But two?

Son: *(Looking at his arm:)*
.....

Mom:
.....

Son:
Exactly, so why did you kidnap me?

Mom:
Who said anything about kidnapping?

Jesus, what will you say next?

What mother
kidnaps her own child?

Son:
I was kidnapped.

You
kidnapped me
by bringing me into this world.

I liked it better
in your womb.

Mom: *(Suddenly enraged:)*
What the hell? I did no such thing!

And if you didn't come out
you would have become blood.

You'd have been wasted, excreted,
mixed with pee
dribbling down my leg.

Son:
I would've disembarked by flowing down your legs
and would have dribbled into the sewer.

What a nice story that would have made...

    Pause.

I could have been trash. Mixed with waste.
But
I became a cripple instead.

    Son looks at his body.

Like this.

Mom:
Why didn't you ask me to kill you
before you were born?

Instead
I birthed you
in times of extreme hardship
and now
this is all you have to say to me?

I don't want someone this ungrateful
to call me on the phone ever again!

Son:
Mom!
I'm here, in front of you,

talking to you in real life.
We aren't on the phone.

We're having a face-to-face
conversation.

Mom:
Sorry, sorry.
I'm losing it.

It's just that it's been years
since I've had a face-to-face
with someone, you know,
a conversation face-to-face,
in person.

Is that how we live now?

Have we become that destitute?

Talking face-to-face.

Son:
Take all my salary! Keep it!

Mom:
What salary? You've never even had a job.

Son:
Oh, sorry, sorry. It's been, been so many
years since I tried to act human. I am losing my mind.

Mom:
Be careful!
Any animal that takes the path of humanity
always results in a scene filled with blood!

Son walks slowly to the refrigerator. Thump, he kicks it with his foot.

Son:
Fuck! Just like a human that thinks he is an animal,
I never recognize the trap.

> *Mom approaches Son and lightly slaps him across the face.*

Mom: *(Smiling:)*
Get your shit straight!

> *Pause.*

> *Mom drags a red bin over to her chair. She cuts her hair and plucks her fur. She begins to shave.*

Son:
Shedding?

Mom:
Yeah. You've gotta do it often to stay close to nature.
It's good for hiding your body.

Son:
Mom, where did dad's molar go?

Mom:
Pawned.

Son:
Fuckers, they swindled us.

> *Pause.*

Son:
::Sniff, sniff::
What's this smell?

Mom:
Your sisters must have gotten scared
and peed on the floor.

Son: *(Keeping his nose shut:)*
This pee smells gross.
It smells like the pee of blind people
that shake when they get scared.

Mom:
You mean like those people
you chewed to death?

You know it won't take them long
to find the bodies.

Soldiers or police,
they'll swarm around the bodies like maggots.

You're afraid of the police, aren't you?

Son:
They've got guns…

Mom:
Those things with your teeth marks,
if they're sent to inspection
you'll be locked away for life.
People with guns
will stick you behind steel bars.
Watch your every move…
So, what would be best
is if you help me.

Son:
But I don't want to.

Mom:
This is a gun.

Bam. Bam. Bam.

Son:
Mom, please, don't make that sound.

I hate guns. I hate the bang.

I lose my shit whenever I hear the bang.

> *Towards the back of the stage, shadow puppets:*
> *A bird flies. Bang. The bird whirls down.*
> *A beast runs. Bang. The beast falls down.*
> *Guns sound. Bang. Guns sound. Bang.*

Alright. I admit there's never a way out with you.
I've got a long way to go before I catch up.

Mom:
There hasn't been a night on earth
where the sound of guns
wasn't heard.

Son:
Or the sound of falling tears.

> *Inside a steel cage—a birdcage—cubs are whining.*
> *Mom approaches the cage to look after the cubs.*

Mom:
Come and say hi.

Son:
No thanks.
You're just going to sell them.
And not for very much either.

Mom:
I'm going to go to the village and get what they're worth!
This time it'll be different.
Look here.
Their eyeballs are already

popping out of their heads.
By the time they're adopted
they'll be all cute and tubby.

   Mom lifts each wolf cub doll up and licks it with her tongue.

Son:
But there's nothing to eat here.
So why do you keep
having babies?

Mom:
There's not much strength left in me.

I can't find food on my own.

These babies
will keep me fed.

Don't be like that, come here and
give their paws a squeeze
before they go away.

Son:
Even if they act super cute,
if they so much as make one mistake
they'll be killed on the spot.

I'll never become a pet like that,
not ever!

Mom: *(Covering the ears of the dolls:)*
Shhh. Your siblings are listening.
If you keep going on like that
I'll slap your ears off.

Son:
I can't hold their hands anyway.

Mom:
Your problem is that you're too negative.

The universe that spills out of you
looks nothing like the one your dad spit out.

Son:
Universe?

Mom:
It's dangerous to enter my universe.

That's what your father said.

Son:
What's that mean?

Mom:
I don't know.

It's hard enough
living on earth.

Son:
When is dad coming home?

Mom:
Your dad isn't coming.
He got abducted in the middle of a street.

Son:
Mom, only children
get kidnapped like that.

Who kidnapped dad?

Mom:
I don't know who they are.

But they must have been from a universe
that is bigger and stronger
than your father's universe.

Son:
Mom,
my universe also grumbles and whines in the night.

Mom:
If that's a thought
you just had
it'll soon slip away.

Son:
It's older than all the funerals in this world.

Mom:
You're your father's son after all.

Saying shit
that makes no sense.

Anyway,
shouldn't you have something to eat?

Then you can help out with the work.

Your face has become half the face it used to be.

Mom puts down the babies.

Son:
Give me some of your milk.

Suddenly, while suckling from Mom's teat.

Shhh!

The sound of hunting dogs barking in the distance.

Mom:
You've been tracked! What will we do!

Mom puts the babies in the cage and perks up her ears.
The barking of hunting dogs gets louder.

Son:
Shit!
They caught our scent!
We've got to make a break for it!

Mom:
It's dangerous!

Outside is full of dogs.

Dogs that die while ripping each other to pieces.

I won't have it.
I won't go.

Son:
Shhh!

Just be quiet.

Mom:
No, no.

I hate dogs.

I hate rats.

Hate. Hate.

The barking of hunting dogs grows louder.

Darkness.

ACT TWO

Wolf cry.

A dark shadow throws money at Mom's side.

The shadow grabs its pants. Puts them on. Disappears.

Mom with her pants half down, sitting on the ground humming a song, counting money with her legs spread in a V.

Son appears with a heaving wolf in his mouth.

Mom:
Ten bucks, twenty bucks, thirty bucks.

She looks at Son.

Son, is that you?

Son: *(Dropping the huffing wolf on the ground with a thump:)*
Yes, mother.

Mom:
Is that really you?
What are you doing home?

> *Son kicks the dead wolf with his foot as he walks over to the rocking chair, where he sits. He opens the freezer. Inside is the head of a baby wolf.*
>
> *Son jams his head in the freezer, and smells the smells, whiff whiff. The head of a smiling pig is sticking out the corner of the freezer. Thwack, he takes it out and drops it to the floor. He bites the pig's head and crams it back in the freezer.*

Son:
Damn.
Somehow I ended up here again.

Mom:
You didn't even call.
Dropping in like this, without warning.
You know, if you had just called
I could have locked the door.

Son:
Mom, can you please pull up your pants.

Mom pulls up her pants.

Mom:
Shhhhh.

Son:
Why?

Mom:
Shut up!
This is just like the last time.
Because of your loudness
you'll get caught again.

Son:
It won't be that easy
for those bastards' hands
to grab hold of me.
Up until now, it's never been easy.

Mom: *(Looking outside:)*
You didn't pee
on the telephone pole near our house
on your way here, did you?
The hunters will
find us. They'll catch us if they whiff
your pee.

Son:
The whole world

doesn't just drop its pants
any damn place like you do.

Mom:
Are you making fun of me?
Just because I
pull down my pants more often than others
doesn't mean I pull down my pants
wherever and whenever I want like you do.

Son:
They won't be able to trace me.
I haven't wailed a single time.

Mom:
Thank God. But what is this shit?

Son:
That? That's for making money. Put it in the freezer.

Mom:
Money? What the hell are you talking about?
You're going to stuff it and sell it?

Son:
I did as you told me to.
At that place
you introduced me to.

Mom:
The duck-hunting place?

Son:
Yes. This time
I really worked my ass off.
When the owner with his hunting rifle
shot down a duck
I ran over like a dog
and placed the duck at his feet.

I worked my ass off
to silence the sound of guns
from this world.

Mom:
Wow, you really acted like a dog.
The owner must have been pleased.
So are you on leave for good behavior?

Son:
I ran away.

Mom:
You didn't bite the owner like a dog again, did you?

Son:
The owner was always yelling at me for being late.
Defective! You are defective!
he would say to me and
some days
I was locked in the cellar
without any water, not even a drop.

Mom:
But you told me the owner pet
your neck and back.

Son:
He grabbed me by my neck
and threw me in the cellar.

Mom:
Imbecile! Didn't I tell you? You must be an animal companion.
You can't betray your owner like some wild bird.

Son:
I didn't betray anyone.
It's just that I couldn't adapt to that life.
I guess I am defective.

Mom:
No, it is those motherfuckers who are the defective ones!
They don't know shit about
shit in this world.
And that is why you ran away, right?

Son:
I don't like fences.

Mom:
I hate fences too.

Son:
Yeah.
I was locked in the cellar
where it was impossible
for me to sleep properly.

I woke up
nightly to the sound, it came from somewhere,
the sound of grinding teeth.
When I woke up
I figured out that the sound of the grinding teeth
belonged to me.

Mom:
Everybody
wakes up at least once
to the sound of their own teeth grinding.
This mother also suffered
when you were gone.
Your siblings all died of hunger.
I wasn't lactating. They had nothing to eat.

Son:
That's because you give your tits
to strange dudes.

Mom:
Stop it. You know I'm ashamed.
But how else can I live?

Son: *(After looking around:)*
How about selling fake milk?
It's better than taxidermy...
Who wants taxidermied animals these days?
Everyone wants a live one.

Mom:
I have no interest in fake milk.

Son:
It's more lucrative
than having kids and putting them up for adoption.

Mom:
Really?
But how does one make breast milk?

Son:
Try going outside.

Because of the nuclear war
there are all kinds of people without parents
wandering the streets.

The young looking anxiously
for their dead mothers
with mouths full of breast milk.

They look up at the sky full of ash and
just before they take their final breath
you must open their mouth with your fingers
and scoop the milk out with a spoon.

Mom:
It's so depressing.

You're going to make me cry.
But why would you say
the milk inside their mouth is fake?

Son:
Because it's half and half.
Half breast milk.
Half tears.

Mom:
There's no profit in it.
I won't do it.

Son:
Mom,
let's be real.

Because of the radiation
your baby-making days
are gone.

In that small amount of time I was away
your butt has become
totally deflated.

Mom:
It'll become juicy again, I know
because I've known hope.

Son:
Hope?

Mom:
Yes, hope. Hope is like
when people stick their empty hands out wide
because they want things.
Or what you think of before sleeping
that brings a smile to your mouth.

Son:
That sounds hard.
I don't understand.

Mom:
It's not time
for you to know hope yet, you're too young.
You'll get it after you've lived longer.
Hope is a thing that you get better at
with age.

Son:
I guess it's like money then.

Mom:
Shit!
How can you be such a good-for-nothing like your father?

Your father, you know he was a poet.
He had very little interest in making money.

Every day
when I was your age
your dad
made me cry.

You know it's a trait of great people.

Only great people have the ability
to make those around them cry.

She laughs.

I guess I only realized it just now…

I spent my days weepily
following your father around.

Son:
Why would you do that?

Mom:
I needed
someone who didn't compromise
their ideals.

Son:
Mom, I promise I won't make anyone
cry.

Mom:
By the sound of it, it seems as though
you're giving up on your ideals.

Son:
Now that I am the age
when you met dad, what should I do then?

Mom:
Make women cry.

Son:
I want to meet a woman
who makes the same sound as me
when I cry.

Mom:
Idiot!
That's not idealism.
Come to your senses.

Are you going to survive
in this harsh world
by climbing on a hill and wailing with your neck stretched out?

Think outside the box.

You have to change your thoughts in order to revolutionize the
world.

The sound of crying
disappears
with the body
the moment you die.

> *Mom puts water in a pot to boil and throws in chunks of meat
> from the refrigerator.*

Son: *(Spitting on the floor and rubbing it around with his foot:)*
Mom, I'm always
wandering around in the blood
I own.

Mom:
I couldn't hear you. Say it again.

Son:
I said, my blood,
I'm wandering around in it.

Mom:
If you want to be with me,
why don't you just put it plainly?

Son:
Sorry.
It's just been so long since I've had a conversation.

> *Mom tastes a ladle of soup to check the seasoning.
> She gives Son a ladle of soup to have him check it too.*

Son: *(Looking at Mom:)*
Left alone
for too long,
the taste is gone.

Mom: *(Hesitating a little:)*
Again. More strange shit dropping out of your mouth.

Who says such things?

You've been out too long
and your ears got soaked
with weird shit.

But at least now that you're here
I'm a little less worried.

I became dejected,
wondering how it was I was going to feed myself.

Son:
Mom, don't worry.

Son kicks the wolf on the floor.

For starters, we have this.

It's the one the owner has had his eyes on
for days.

Even if you shoot at him
he is the kind of animal that doesn't run.

Every night he paced near
the cellar where I was locked up.

The owner wanted to catch him,
so he took me out of the cellar
to use me as bait.

He said if the beast is hungry
it'll even eat a young thing like me,
so he dragged me by the nape of my neck
out to the hunting field.

Mom comes closer to take a look at the wolf.

Mom:
So you stole
the thing your owner loved.

I can only imagine
how much we will get after we stuff him!

Son:
I will take cotton
and stuff it in his organs.

The beast will be
warmer
and softer inside
than it was in life.

Mom:
Quickly now, since we're hungry,
let's cut it open. Eat some fresh meats.

Son: *(Drool flowing out his mouth:)*
Before it rots!

Mom:
Let's dig in!

Mom grabs a kitchen knife.

Son:
There was still breath left
in him when I ran over
after he'd been shot, so
I did as you taught me.
I bit his neck
to end his life.
It was my last chance
to leave a good impression

on the owner.
I did it exactly as you taught me.
I didn't look into his eyes
and got it over quickly.

Mom:
That's right.
You've really got to give the jugular a snap
so it can't move.

*Mom comes near and flips the wolf over so she can split its belly
with a knife.
She gives it a once-over.*

Mom:
Son?

Son:
Yes.

Mom:
It's got bedsores. There are too many
sores to stuff it.
Turn it over on its belly.

Son:
Why its belly?

Mom:
Because this asshole,
it's one that I feel like I've seen many times before.

Son flips the wolf onto its belly without getting up from his chair.

Mom stumbles back in surprise when she sees the wolf.

Son:
What's the matter?

Mom:
Son! How can this be?

Son:
What's the matter?

Mom:
No…

Son:
What?

Mom:
Son, this is your father.

Son:
How can that be?

Mom,
I have never even met
my father.

Mom:
The beast lying in front of you,
this is your father.

Son:
But you said that dad
was one who wandered
the forest…

Mom:
You killed your father.

Son:
But you said whenever
dad came for you, he did it
with his asshole dilating.

Mom:
You killed your father.

Son:
Mom,
I've never killed my father before.

Mom:
Same here.

Who's killed their father?

What kind of person does that?

Tell me,
what does it feel like?
Killing your father?

Son looks around confused.

Son:
Mom, this is a really big deal.
I killed dad.

We should report the murderer to the police.

Mom:
Are you planning to have me starve to death?

There's no law that says we have to report you, is there?

Let's not act too hastily
and think of a different way.

At this moment Woman opens the door and enters.

Woman:
Fuck!

It's too damn cold
for me to wait any longer.

How long do I have to squat
with my mouth open
outside?

Are you planning to have me starve to death?

Jesus, and just a few minutes ago
you were telling me
how warmly you wanted to embrace me.

> *Woman comes into the room and opens the refrigerator.*

> *A stuffed head pops out.*

> *The refrigerator is full of things to eat.*

> *She eyes Mom and shuts the door with a slam.*

Mom:
Do you want to end up in there too?

Son, who is this woman here?

Son:
That's the woman I plan to live with.

We met in the sewer.

When I said I was lonely
she opened her crotch for me.

Woman:
If you're lonely
you can come inside me.

Inside here

is the deepest
void in the world.

Mom:
You lowly motherfucker.

Look at that crotch.

That crotch is a swamp.

Son:
But when loneliness comes
it is the warmest swamp.

Mom:
Is that all you've got to say?

You are really pathetic.

Worse than
an animal that dies
in a trap on the road.

Son embraces Woman.

Son:
Go ahead, say hi to Mother.

Woman:
Hello Mother.

Mom:
It smells like a fucking rat.

Son! It smells like rats in this house.

Traps. We must lay traps.

Mom throws rat traps around Woman.

Woman:
Cunt bitch!

Son:
Mom! Stop it!

Mom:
The whole house
smells like dirty rat.

Rat.

Rat smells everywhere.

Haven't you heard?

All the rats abandon
a ship before it sinks.

So, think about it, how did they get
on the ship in the first place?

Woman: *(Steps on a trap:)*
Ow!

Mom:
Got one!

Son:
Please stop!

Woman:
Cunt bitch!

> *Son brings a bucket of water and begins washing Woman's feet by licking them with his tongue.*

Mom:
So?

Where is it exactly you think you two were going to live?

Son:
I thought we'd stay here.

It's too cold
for us to go outside again.

Mom:
You're insane.

You know we can't live with a rat.

It's cramped and smelly here.
Also, there's no light.

Son:
I guess if there are only two people
living here, it won't be cramped.

It wasn't cramped before when it was just us two.

And anyway, it would be rude of me
to live here after killing dad.

Mom:
Why do you think you are being rude by staying?

This mother of yours
is old now and too feeble to find food.

Son:
You are a bad woman!

Mom:
How can you say something like that
to your mother?

Son:
Because this woman
told me that I must say
these words to my mother.

Mom:
Why?

Son:
Because there is a child
growing
inside that woman's belly.

Mom stares intensely at Woman.

Mom:
You rat-faced bitch!

Woman:
I wanted to erase it,
but he begged me not to.

He said something about
his universe wandering around
here and there
inside my belly.

Just like the other times,
I'll go to the bathroom right away
and try to get rid of it.

Just like the last time...

Son:
You can't do that.

You can't just take a universe
into the bathroom
and flush it away!

Woman:
What is your universe anyway?

Is it so precious?

Son:
It's the sound of a cry.

Woman:
The sound of a cry, ha.

If you wrap it
in toilet paper
and throw it away
who will ever know?!

Son:
Our bodies
are like toilet paper.

Toilet paper that gets thrown out
after spending its life
wiping the soul completely.

Woman: *(Grabbing Son by the nape of his neck:)*
Come to your senses, you cripple.

We don't even have the money to buy toilet paper.

Son:
What?
What about all that toilet paper I brought you?

Woman:
Every day
I used it up
wiping the tears
you made people cry.

Son:
What about the toilet paper
we collected off the street?

Woman:
I used it all up
wiping up all that blood
that came pouring out of
your nose,
the blood that came from all the times
people beat you up
after you read your poems out loud.

Son:
At least we
still have the bird.

I've heard that gynecologists
secretly wrap young birds in rags
and throw them out
at night.

    Son touches Woman's belly.

Little birdy, little birdy! Cry for Daddy! Cry for Daddy!
Flap the arms I gave you!

    Woman looks at her stomach.
    She giggles. She sniffles.
    Just like a rat.

Mom: *(Grabbing Son and taking him into a corner:)*
You have to erase it.

Do you want to give birth
to a cripple like you?

Son:
This child, the child that looks like my two arms,

he will be born.

Mom:
Erase it!

Before she gets morning sickness,
have her eat a live mamushi
or python.

Make sure it has poison
so that the baby
bites down on its tongue
and chokes to death.

But if that doesn't work...

Woman:
Oh! Mother! How did your tongue get so twisted!

Son:
Mom, it is impossible
to kill the sound of a cry
inside a belly.

That child makes
the same cry as me
because it was me
that put the baby inside
that woman's belly.

Mom:
If it is born,
you won't even be able to hug it.

Son:
Even so, it will
be a thing I will never be able to look at
eye to eye. Just like with you... Mom.

Mom:
I don't
want anyone to call me grandmother.

Son:
Even so, now is the time
I must become a dad.

Mom:
You say such childish things…
just like your father.

Fathers are nothing but taxidermied animals.

Idiotically, with their eyes raised high in the sky,
they pretend like they have dignity,
but they're not useful for anything.
Your children, no,
the cries you think are like your cries
will disappear from this world
as soon as they are hungry.

> *The sound of sirens ring outside.*
> *Policemen in cyber suits rush in the house.*
>
> *They begin to search the house, flipping furniture over.*
> *They take their barcode scanner and scan the corpse.*

Policeman 2: *(Holding his nose:)*
Eugh. That smell.

I can't breathe through my nose.

I think I'm going to have to breathe
through my asshole.

Mom:
Officers, I only sell
dead things caught in traps

or hit by cars on the road.

Policeman 2:
We are well-trained personnel.

Policeman 1:
This is it.
This is the thing
that was filed as missing yesterday.

Policeman 2:
Yeah?

> *Policeman 2 looks around at Mom, Son, and Woman.*

> *Mom opens the refrigerator door.*
> *Mom takes out a wad of cash and hides it in her purse.*
> *It looks like she is getting ready to make a break for it.*

Policeman 2:
Wait, you there without arms.
Come here! Open your mouth!

> *Son opens his mouth for the officer.*
> *Policeman 1 shines a flashlight on his teeth.*
> *Policeman 2 takes out a wanted suspect photo,*
> *looks at it, then Son's face, then the picture,*
> *and it appears as though*
> *he's just confirmed something.*

> *Policemen 1 and 2 whisper together.*

Policeman 2:
Yes. Those are the canines we've been looking for.
But where did he hide his molars?

> *On her way out the door Mom stops, puts down the bag, and*
> *turns around.*

Mom:
Mr. Policeman, Sir,
everyone in this family
lives each day of their lives
biting down their molars.

Look, why don't we go over there...
And I'll pull down my pants....
Please, just let us go, just this once.

Policeman 1:
You're under arrest
for murder and dismemberment
and the illegal sale
of the organs of a blind family
on the black market.

> *Policeman 1 goes behind Son
> and tries to put cuffs on him.*
>
> *Son growls.
> Mom approaches Son and hugs him tight.*

Mom:
But my son
hasn't done anything.

My son
didn't kill anyone.

There is no proof.

Policeman 1:
Maybe so, maybe not.

All will be revealed
in the investigation.

Son:
I'm being framed!

This is an honorable house!

Policeman 1:
I have no interest in your ramblings.
I mean look here. I've got a gun!

There's never been a day
where the sound of guns vanished on earth.

Son:
There's nothing I hate more in this world than guns.

I swear, I'm innocent!

Woman snarls and rushes at the police.

Woman:
AAAAAAAAH!

*Policeman 1 brings down the butt of his gun
on Woman's head.*

Policeman 1:
Obstructing official police business.
Space dust, 6 months for you!
And 2 years of life without gravity!

*The policemen throw around and flip things over in the house.
They wrinkle their noses.*

Policeman 1:
You people, you disgust me.

I want to shoot
up
everything.

He points his gun at Mom.

You're suspicious too.
Families are always in on each other's plans.

Woman:
After the nuclear bomb fell
all the families disappeared
from the world.

Don't you know?

Policeman 2:
Even zombies
miss humans so much
they stuff
the corpses of people they find
in the dark.

I mean who can really know how many people
are still alive...

So answer me clearly!

Are you human or are you animal?

> *Policemen 1 and 2 lift their guns and aim them at each person.*
> *Son is scared.*
> *Mom is scared.*
> *Woman is scared.*

Woman:
I am a rat.
That woman over there,
she forced us into this mess.

Mom: *(Flinching:)*
Mr. Policeman, officers, we are a nuclear family.
From time to time we see each other.

That child,
when he was young,
he was a good and innocent child.

Mom tears up suddenly.

That dear boy,
aside from having no arms,
he's completely normal.
He left his arm inside me
but he's worked hard to care for his dear mother.

Sirs, officers, the crying the boy does
is a kind of instinctual self-defense.

That child thinks
he can cry
and give his tears to
all those in the world
so they need never cry.
His mind's not right.
Take him away,
quickly please… ::sniff:: ::sniff::

Policeman 2 brings over a stuffed animal.

Policeman 2:
Taxidermy…
People who have the desire
to go into the business of creating
lifeless objects
are usually one of two kinds.
They are either artists
or criminals.
In the case of your son…

Mom:
My son is both. I weep.
::sniffle:: ::sniffle::

Policeman 2:
I see, well considering this situation,
we'll first have to arrest
your son's psychological state.

The failure of beasts
to maintain the noise of their cry
is also a failure of beasts
to preserve their tribe.

It looks as if your son
wanted a slightly different way
to do research on *The Origin of Species*.

But we with guns,
we must detect psychological states
before they leave normality,
and detain them.

That's what we are trained for.

Mom:
You're right.
From the first to the last page,
my son memorized *The Origin of Species*.

From a very young age
I trained him
to flip the pages with his toes.

My boy can also count money
with his toes.

If you need evidence,
he can demonstrate right here, right now.

Son, what are you doing?
Come here right now.

Policeman 1:
That's unnecessary!

If you have evidence, you can
send it via email or letter.

Policeman 2:
TNT 6071!

This mother and son,
they are like languages that live
in one another's background.

It's suspicious.

Policeman 1:
You're right.

They're like the background
that floats
between one another's language.

They're not really acting like humans or animals,
but more like language.

It's been so long since language disappeared
from this world,
how is it that there are still those that use it?

Language is forbidden!

You are all sentenced to space dust!

Search around!
They might be reading books!

It's suspicious!

Son:
There are no such things as books here.

Why would we ever look at printed letters?

How would we ever get our hands on such a thing?

You know as well as I do that there are more satellites than books.

Woman:
Mister, this man's destiny has no shame.

His fate walks around here and there,
overturning false accusations, taking the blame for them.

He said the only thing that he saw inside of books
were sewers.

Policeman 2:
Books? Did you say he saw books?

If you did, that means
they're using language!

You are sentenced!
200 years of space dust!

Policeman 1 takes aim at Son.

Son:
It's been so many years now since we lost language.

I was born after language disappeared.

I'm a wolf.

Policeman 2:
Come on bro, let's take these people
back into orbit.

Policeman 1:
Hey.
Didn't I already tell you?
Don't call me bro in public?

We're cyber machines for God's sake.
Straighten out your act!

Woman:
You've got to take them all away.
It's cramped here
even for an old woman like me, alone.
::sniffle:: ::sniffle::

Policeman 2:
Don't squeak.

We might cut your tail off.

Suddenly Son stands up, completely at peace.

Son:
Mom, it's time for me to go.
I'll take the blame.

Be healthy
till I return.

And take good care of this woman
and our child.

Mom:
Alright.

Next time don't forget to call
before you come to visit.

Policeman 1 again tries to cuff Son.
Reaffirming that he has no arms,

Policeman 1 becomes a little alarmed.

Policemen 1 & 2:
There's no cause for alarm.

We are trained professionals.

We are series TNT21-22.
We've been constructed
and programmed to understand
people and their interpersonal relationships.

If you move more than five kilometers
without this barcode
the self-destruct mechanism planted
inside your internal organs
will activate and blow you up.

Once our commands are carried out
we send the pixelated evidence of our actions
until the corporation confirms
that we have fulfilled the provisions of our contract.

We mustn't
trust people.

Scarier than trust, is to
love.

We have been educated in the training
of how not to love.

Son:
I'm sorry I don't have arms for you to cuff.

Policeman 2:
Right, no arms to cuff. Too bad.

However, many fates change

after hands are cuffed.

And you
don't even have palms to read.

So no one can read your future.

Son smiles.

Woman gets up.

Woman:
Travel safely darling!

Son:
Yes, of course, honey.

Do a good job birthing.

Don't drool
everywhere you go!

Woman:
Yes, I promise. From now on I won't squeak.
Goodbye, darling.

Son rubs his face against the belly of Woman.

Mom:
Get away
from my offspring!

You rat!

Woman:
Bitch!

Woman looks at Son.

What're you waiting for!
Tell your mother
exactly what I told you to say.

Son:
Be quiet!

Son shakes off the policemen and kicks Woman.

The policemen stop him.

Son:
Mom?

Mom:
What is it, son?

Son:
Mom, continually in this life, why are we growing thin?

Mom:
Son, even if things grow more dim,
remember that when you were born
it was me who licked
you.

Son:
Mom, even if I see a light,
I won't rush to it anymore.

Mom:
Son, don't go around
leaving blood on the street.
When people see your blood,
the volume of their footsteps turns to low.

Policeman 1:
Take him away!

Policeman 2:
If I hear anymore,
I might get infected by their language.

He takes a walkie-talkie from his pocket to make a transmission.

Roger! This is planet B289. Codename
Earth. 4800AD. TNT21-22.
It seems all surviving humans
have headed to the archives.
We did not see any iron men
between buildings. No first generation
robots like Eva 1 were present. There hasn't
been a single earthquake since 2096.
We couldn't determine whether
the defensive HQ is underground
or hidden deep under a nearby ocean.
After receiving orders to find the RCA receiving tube
which hasn't been manufactured since 1954,
we've come through Ikebukuro and arrived at Akihabara.
Currently it is 4 degrees, the time
is 11PM, 200% humidity, and the space
between buildings is full of movement,
maybe human, maybe replicant.
Types of living organisms: humans,
wolves, ghosts, rats. The vampires
are asleep behind the buildings.
In 2067 this city was overrun by zombies.
Eventually they ran out of food
and for the next 1500 years
zombies ate other zombies
until they died out.
The sky is changing
from gray to black lead. It's time
to eat the capsule. We'll fly back soon.
In order to survive, the creatures here live
without opening their mouths. The laughing virus
made the humans laugh and they kept laughing
until they went extinct.

On Earth there are still charges that
the subjects of the "YOU NO MORE" authority
experiment were humans.
It appears as if we have found cases
of "language" (forbidden in space)
being used.
Here the buildings corrode quickly
the moment wet air touches them.
Maybe they had not invented a device
to record and analyze this, because the
speed of corrosion of everything in this city is high.
Preparing for departure, Roger.

Somewhere outside a spaceship lands with a loud boom.

Son:
Wait, officer, sir.
If this is my last meeting with my mother,
can't you let us, you know, have some time
alone together?

Policeman 2:
Ten minutes.
No more.

Son:
Yes, ten minutes is enough.
To pound the rice into a cake. Yes.

Mom, quick!
Without me here
you will starve to death!

Policeman 1:
We'll be waiting outside.
Finish quickly.

Mom:
Yes, we've got to do it hastily.

Let us see if your skills have improved.

I will give you rice cakes
and you will spit on my body.

Before my ass shrivels any more,
I must make rice cakes at least once more.

Son bites Mom by the butt.

Mom:
Ah, ah........... Hurtssssso good.

Son:
It's still plump enough.
Mom, there is hope.

Mom:
Hope. What is hope?

Son:
It's that brief moment, together,
the brief moment before sleeping together.

Mom and Son go into a room.
An outline of their shadows can be seen having sex.

Son, as if he is taking the words he wants to say and penetrating
them into the deepest part of Mom,
Mom, as if she is taking in the words one at a time deep in her
body.
Some dirt crumbles and falls from the ceiling.
As if gasping, as if crumbling, slowly.

Little by little the music booms.

Son:
Mom?

Mom:
What is it?

Son:
If stuffed animals
don't have a crying sound,
why don't they rot?

Mom:
I mean why don't fish cry? Why can't rocks be taxidermied?
I want to stuff clouds and sell them in a foreign country.
We should pack and ship snow to Africa instead of food.
Since no one has ever seen snow, it'll make money.
Why can't snow be taxidermied?

Mom and Son smile.

Son:
Mom, I feel as if
I'm still breathing heavily
inside your body.

Give me back my arm.

Mom:
That story again... and again... enough . . .

I'm telling you, it's not here.

Son:
I know it's here.

Mom:
Go and look for it somewhere else.

Son: *(Feeling down below:)*
Here, here.

Mom:
Don't finish.
Don't finish.

Son:
Mom, I
have the same blood as you, right?

Mom:
No, I don't want to share
my blood with you.

The only thing we share is the sound
of our cry.

Slowly.
Do it slowly.
I can't understand it.

Son:
I've established communication with my arm.
My crying is
the crying of my handicap.
I am calling my handicap.
Mom,
I wasn't
::pant:: ::pant:: born...
without an arm...

Mom:
That story again, ::pant:: ::pant::
can't you stop
saying it?

Son:
I left here,
here
I left my arm.
I left it here.

Mom:
::pant:: ::pant:: Hold on a bit.
Maybe because you've been out there wandering, maybe
your strength is not what it used to be.
How can a man have a universe
if he doesn't even have the stamina to please his mother?
Spit on my body.
Drool on me.
You left it here.
That arm. Inside my body.
You left it here.

Son:
::pant:: ::pant:: I can't hold it much longer.
Strange roots are pulling me.

Mom:
Just a bit more, harder…

Son:
Ugh….

Mom:
Just a bit…

Son:
Mom…
Mom!
Mom!

Mom:
Stop,
Stop, ah…
It hurts. It hurts.

Son:
Ugh… I really can't.
What do I do?

Mom:
Spill it. In me...
Spill it in me.

Son:
Really, can I spill
inside you?

Mom:
Yes, spill in me,
in me....
Spill it all. Do it.

Son:
Ugh!

Mom: *(Screaming as if her body is full of water:)*
AHHHHHHH

> *Woman lifts her head again, suddenly opening her eyes.*

Woman:
AR AR AR ARMM ARMMM ARMMM SOAKKE
SOAKKEED
AR AR AR ARMM ARMMM ARRMMMMM WETTT
WETTTT
AR AR AR ARMMM ARMMM ARRMMMM .... CRY
CRY CRYING
ARRR ARR ARM ARM ARM ARM COME COMING
COMING OUT

> *After a while the light comes back on.*

> *Outside, signs of the policemen.*

Policeman 1: *(Voice:)*
Come on out.
It's time for the gate to close.

If you don't come back now
you'll be trapped in time forever.

Outside the door, the blue light of the spaceship is everywhere.

Son limps out.

Mom: *(Coming to her senses:)*
You're just like your father.

From a young age
full of so many oddities.

The policemen are busy, but
shouldn't you get going too?

I'll open the door.

Son:
Yes, Mom,
thank you.

Mom opens the door.
The police open Son's mouth
and take cans from out their pockets and spray Son's mouth with
frost.

Son's mouth gets frozen solid.
Son is muzzled.
He is led out.

The sound of a gun, bam!

Mom shuts the door and seems lost in thought.
Somewhere, a long howl from a wolf.
Mom opens her legs and looks down between them.

A wolf howls from deep inside her womb.

Mom falls backwards.

Darkness.

ACT THREE

*Woman sits on the rocking chair and occasionally looks down at
her belly.*

She reads a storybook to the child in her belly..

Woman:
A faint, monotonous, clear, but faraway bell
rings from the distance. The sunlight
bites the faraway ring of the bell in its mouth and goes away.
My language deepens in the night so that you
become the shade of beasts. And when dawn breaks, the shade
of plants. At night my language becomes a beast. And at dawn,
a plant. What am I talking about? I want to say
that some lives don't die by vomiting blood, but
by vomiting all the plants inside their bodies.
You, remember, humans always worry about the part
instead of the whole, and then they go.
You, remember, the time pointing toward you
has always been animal or plant, I am
now polluting the environment that lives inside me. You
are a barbarian and I am the infinite masks
domesticated by time. You are a guest, so come on in.

> *One slow ring of the doorbell.*
> *Mom enters wearing black sunglasses and carrying a cane.*

> *Woman hides her storybook behind her back.*
> *Mom comes near, feeling along the wall.*

Woman:
Oh, mother!

Mom:
Yes, child…

> *Mom feels along the wall and looks around*
> *as though she can't see in front of her face.*

Woman:
What are you doing home
so suddenly?
You didn't even call…
If I'd had a man here
that would have been a big deal, no?

Mom: *(Coughing:)*
You changed your number again.

Woman:
It's too cramped in
here for two people.

  Mom hobbles over to the rocking chair and sits.

Mom:
Did you hear any news about him?

Woman:
Not yet.

Mom:
My son, I mean.

Woman:
That story again.
Mom, I'm sick of it now.
It's been almost a year
since he got on that spaceship.

Mom:
My son was kidnapped,
and taken to a distant universe.

Woman:
Aren't you sick of this shit?

I want to stop

discussing it.

He ran off into the woods
and rambled
and froze to death in a trap.

Mom:
My son wrote poetry.

Woman:
Mom, how many times do I have to tell you?
That's just what you think happened.
He was just a cripple.

Mom:
When I tried to erase that child
I clearly heard the scream
of my son in my gut.

Woman:
Mom, life
is full of screams.

Everyday you hear at least one.

Didn't you know?

Mom:
Those
are the last words
my son left
inside your mouth.

Woman:
Yes. He
always muttered
crazy words
right before he left.

Mom:
Now I,
I am crying.

Not speaking those words.

Woman approaches Mom.

Woman:
Mother, give me a hug.

Harder.

Mother, are you planning to have me starve?

This child in my belly
is going to die with an empty mouth.

Now come to your senses
and work.

How much did you get this time?

Mom takes the money out of her basket and gives it to Woman.

Mom:
I'm sorry.

But I can't work
anymore.

I'm old and feeble.

Woman:
At this rate
my asshole will shrivel up.

It would be better to get stuffed and taxidermied
rather than live another moment with this hunger.

Mom:
Did you already use up
the money I brought you
last time?

Woman:
Mother,
it's already
been a month.

Mom:
What about the money
I got begging
on the subway?

Woman:
I used it up
buying your sunglasses.

Mom:
What about the money
I got squatting
on the bridge?

Woman:
I used it to buy
your harmonica.

Mom:
Look, I
want to rest now.

Mom plops down.

Woman:
Mother,
how will you make it in this world
if you give up on everything so easily?

Maybe it's time for you to help out at home
instead of rambling about.

Remember, it was you who wanted to work the streets.

> *Mom gets up from the chair.*
> *She goes toward the door feeling around with her cane.*

Mom:
My son rambles around the forest.

Let's keep the door open
in case he comes back.

Woman:
Anything that rambles around
because it misses this world
is a ghost.

Mom:
Child…

Woman:
Now what?

Mom:
It's not that I've lost
my eyes.

It's that I can't
open them.

Woman:
Mom, at night
my universe also groans.

> *Mom's cough deepens.*
> *She stops in her tracks while opening the door.*

Mom:
Is the baby in your belly
growing healthy?

Woman:
A few days ago
it developed one ear.
It developed a toe.
It listens to the outside sounds a bit
and drums on my belly from inside.

Mom:
Wolves are bred from the eyes.
I read that in
many a fairytale.

Woman:
Fairytales
are adult nightmares.
I won't read such things
to my child.

Mom:
When you
are all grown,
I want to lose my way
with you at my side.

Woman:
Mother, those are the words
your son said to my stomach
for the baby.

Mom:
Yes, yes.
Thank you.

Woman approaches Mom and lightly slaps her across the face.

Woman:
Come to your senses.

You're just like him,
saying crazy things
no one can understand.

You must be busy.

I'll open
the door for you.

Mom:
Okay, alright.

Woman:
When you come back,
don't forget to call first.

Mom:
I know.
I won't forget this time.

> *Mom exits through the door*
> *and Woman closes the door. There is momentary silence.*
> *Woman sits in the chair. She picks up the fairytale book again.*
> *Woman looks down at her stomach.*
> *Woman suddenly begins dry heaving.*

Woman:
Has it been twenty months already?
Why does it not even try to come out?!
Even though it's way past
when it was expected!
It won't stop crying inside me!
Every night the child's crying
flows out between my legs!
Shut up!
Shut up!

There is nothing this strange.
I feel like I'm holding it
in my gut.

> *Woman goes to the corner and sits on the pee pot.*
> *She's straining her sphincter. Her expression strains too.*
> *As if deciding it won't do, she goes to the sink and gets out a bottle.*
> *In the bottle there is a live mamushi coiled up.*
> *She lifts the bottle, about to drink.*

> *The volume heightens.*
> *Falling clumps of white dirt.*

> *From somewhere, the sound of a howl reverberates.*
> *Like every cry that lives inside the womb of this world.*

> *Suddenly*
> *Mom kicks down the door and rushes at Woman.*

Mom:
No!
I can see it! I can see it!

> *Exploding out, the long howl of a wolf.*

> *Slowly, lights dim to black.*

END

BORN A (MAN)IMAL
ON KIM KYUNG JU'S *BRED FROM THE EYES OF A WOLF*

I.

The background of Kim Kyung Ju's *Bred from the Eyes of a Wolf* is a pastiche of dystopian worlds. The earth has suffered a nuclear holocaust, zombies have almost eaten the entirety of the living, and because of the lack of food, the zombies turned on each other, resorting to zombie cannibalism. Even though most traces of life have been wiped out, survival is still dependent on a market economy dictated by the exchange of capital. In this way familiar mythologies and science fictions are layered one over the other in order to create the conditions in which the reigning ideology of contemporary capitalism can be put on display. Slavoj Žižek was right when he said it is much easier to imagine the end of the world than the end of capitalism. However, even though they do not provide us with direct answers to current crises, only in the absence of the world do dystopian narratives help reveal aspects of capitalism that might one day help us move beyond it. As Fredric Jameson has argued, this is why dystopian allegory is so important. It contains within it a utopian promise. In this way we can read the inversion of Kim's pastiche dystopia as a pastiche of utopian possibility.

II.

Although familiar in many ways, *Bred from the Eyes of a Wolf* is not a simple story of human survival after the apocalypse.

> *In an age of collision and blended time,*
> *after the atomic war,*
> *species intermingle*
> *and resemble other species.*

By staging the animal-as-human or human-as-animal, wolves that think and feel like humans or humans that feel and think like wolves, the audience is asked to question what the qualifiers are which separate humans from animals. Kim has written that the human-wolves that appear in the play are more or less the same as any petit-bourgeois family we might find in Korea today. Inspiration for the concept came when he read an article about a woman who began to sell her children's organs on the black market. In this way this play does not so much present a dystopian future in which people and animals are indistinguishable so much as an allegorical representation of the degraded social relations of the present.

The family that appears in the story consists of a son who has lost both his arms, the father who abandoned the family to become a poet vagabond, and the mother who has resorted to killing, taxidermying, and selling her offspring in order to make ends meet. The family structure has been reduced to pure economic relations. The male body has become partitioned off into monetized parts and the female body has become useful only for its reproductive ability.

Mom:
Your dad
lost nine of his toes
in the jerky factory
trying to keep us fed.

Son:
One a year!

Mom:
Yes, and sometimes one every six months.

Son:
That was your idea, wasn't it!

To have dad put his foot
into the machines.

Claim injury compensation.

You know, even now it seems
like such an excellent plan.

Mom is pleased, shakes her ass.

Mom:
Yes.

If it wasn't for that plan
we would have all
starved to death.

The role of the male in the family is to sacrifice his body for the family. The mother thinks that the father ran away because "Your father, you know he was a poet. / He had very little interest in making money." However, we can imagine another reason the father left the family is that his fate would be to sacrifice parts of himself until there was literally nothing of him left. This mirrors the overworked father figure that has become a staple character in popular Korean culture: the father who feels like he is sacrificing his life and body for the economic survival of the family. However, the father—unlike the mother—has the freedom to escape. The mother is tied to a domestic situation. She lives inside a symbol for the family (tree), and is forced to make a life from selling her body through prostitution and child-bearing.

In a twist of the Oedipal myth, the son accidentally kills his own father without realizing it. He takes the corpse back to his mother who recognizes it as the body of the father.

Mom:
You killed your father.

Son:
Mom,
I've never killed my father before.

Mom:
Same here.

Who's killed their father?

What kind of person does that?

Tell me,
what does it feel like?
Killing your father?

Son looks around confused.

Son:
Mom, this is a really big deal.
I killed dad.

We should report the murderer to the police.

Just as in the Oedipal myth, the son ends up copulating with the mother after killing the father. However, like the mother taxidermying her own offspring, because the characters in the play are half-human half-animal, the audience is presented with an ethical problem. If these are animals, do we judge these acts to be grotesque? If these are humans, are the characters any less gruesome for what they have done? If the thought of humans killing their own offspring is horrific, is the thought of animals doing it any less so? Can we ask the same question about incest? Is it because we tend to think of animals as having less interiority than humans, less of a moral compass, that we consider ourselves superior? Is it because we think humans have a richer inner life? This final question is addressed through the symbolic exploration of the inner universe that lives inside and is passed down from the father and son.

Son:
Mom,
my universe also grumbles and whines in the night.

Mom:
If that's a thought
you just had
it'll soon slip away.

Son:
It's older than all the funerals in this world.

Mom:
You're your father's son after all.

Saying shit
that makes no sense.

The internal universe of the father and son is articulated through poetic aphorism. For the mother, the only language that makes any sense is one of crude economic relations. The material of poetry, language, is free. This inherently makes it hard to value in terms of economic relations. This is why the father leaves the family in order to live his life as a wandering poet. He feels trapped in a world driven by market value. However, because he cannot escape capitalist hegemony, eventually the father is caught by a hunter. Marx wrote, "The bourgeoisie has stripped of its halo every occupation hitherto honored and looked up to with reverent awe. It has converted the physician, the lawyer, the priest, the poet, the man of science, into its paid wage laborers." The capitalist society creates a system which is ubiquitous. Once entered into the system, one never escapes alienation. Not even the path of the poet is sacred. However, if there is any promise of freedom, it exists privately. Where one is not free in the world, they must create a universe of freedom in their inner-life. This is the dichotomy that is represented throughout the play with the symbolic rendering of the internal/external universe.

Even after the son is taken away by the cyborg policemen for some kind of Orwellian crime, his child remains inside the womb of a woman he brought home. The cry that exists in the child yet to be born is the continuation of the universe being passed down from father to son to grandchild. When the play ends, the mom says "I can see it! I can see it!" And a long wolf cry is heard as the lights fade to black. What is immortal then is not the taxidermied progeny of the mother (the commodity) but the ineffable and transient traces of inner freedom (the wolf howl).

It is important that the howl does not take place in language—as a word within a grammatical system. It is the ur-text of the animal inside the human. Paradoxically, the language which represents what is most human (our inner-life) is the wolf's scream.

— Jake Levine, 2017

WORKS CITED

Adorno, Theodor W., and Max Horkheimer. *Dialectic of Enlightenment*. London: Verso, 2016. Print.

Benjamin, Walter. *The Origin of German Tragic Drama*. London: Verso, 2009. Print.

Freud, Sigmund, and Peter Gay. *The Freud Reader*. New York: W.W. Norton &, 1995. Print.

Jameson, Fredric. *Valences of the Dialectic*. London: Verso, 2010. Print.

Marcuse, Herbert. *One-dimensional Man: Studies in the Ideology of Advanced Industrial Society*. London: Routledge, 2008. Print.

Marx, Karl, Friedrich Engels, and Samuel Moore. *The Communist Manifesto*. Harmondsworth: Penguin, 1967. Print.

Many of **KIM KYUNG JU'S** books have been translated into English and published in the English speaking world. These include *I Am a Season That Does Not Exist in the World* (Black Ocean, 2016), *Whale and Vapor* (Black Ocean, 2019), and *Butterfly Sleep* (Tupelo Press, 2019). Kim has been the recipient of many prestigious awards in Korea, including the Kim Su-young prize and Today's Young Artist Prize.

JAKE LEVINE is a writer and translator and has received various awards and grants for his poetry and translation including a Fulbright scholarship and a KGSP scholarship. He is an assistant professor of Creative Writing at Keimyung University and teaches stylistics at the Korean Literature Translation Academy.